I Am the Sun

House of Lore

REBECCA AND JAMES MCDONALD

I look like a giant, fiery ball burning bright in the sky, but I'm actually a star, like some of the stars you see twinkling far off in the night sky. Scientists call me a yellow dwarf star.

Not all nebulae grow stars, but for the nebulae that do, they usually have many stars coming to life inside them, so I probably have sisters and brothers shining bright in outer space.

Even though I'm round like planet Earth, I don't have a hard surface to land on. I'm mostly made up of two important gases called Hydrogen and Helium.

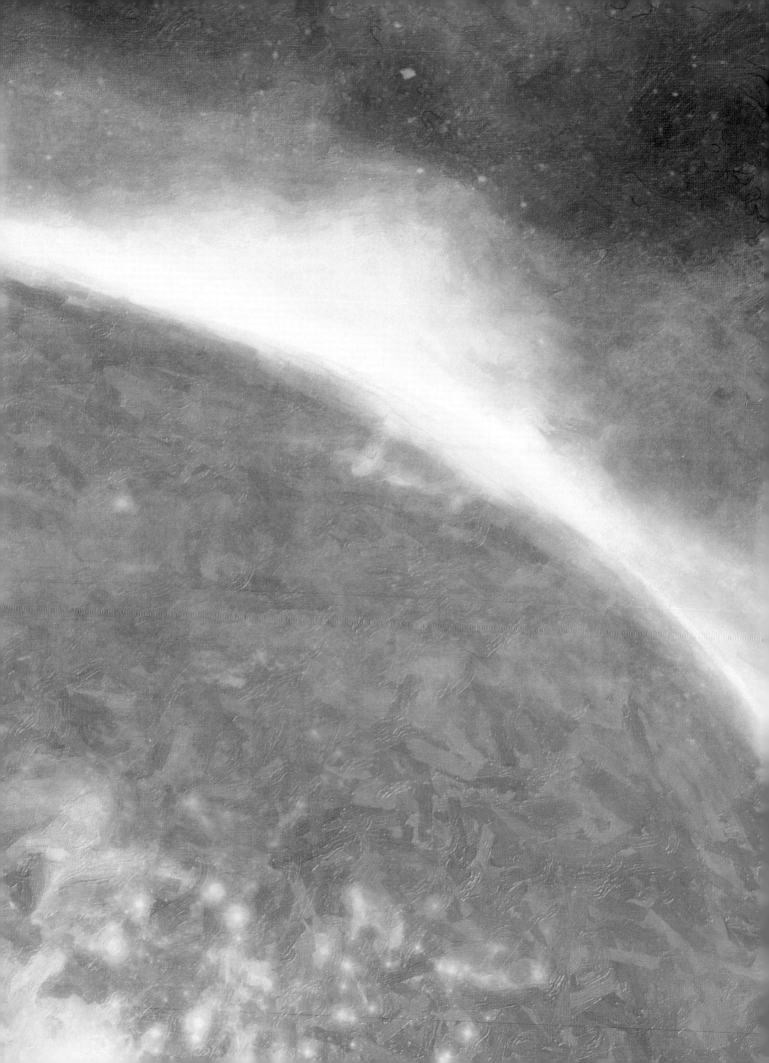

And when people and animals eat plants, guess whose energy makes it all possible. That's right! It's me, the Sun. Even the weather is affected by the energy I give off.

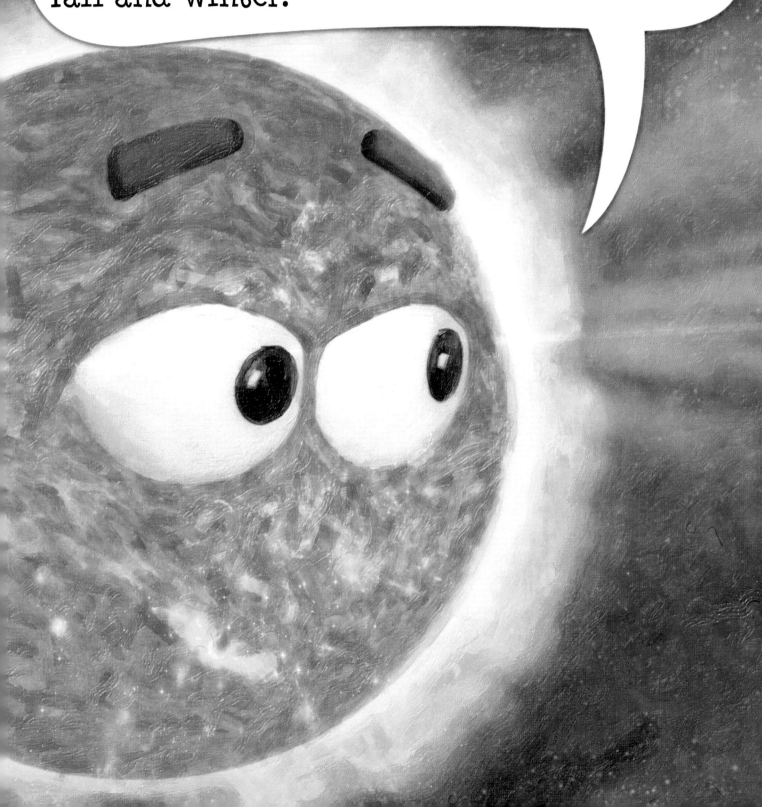

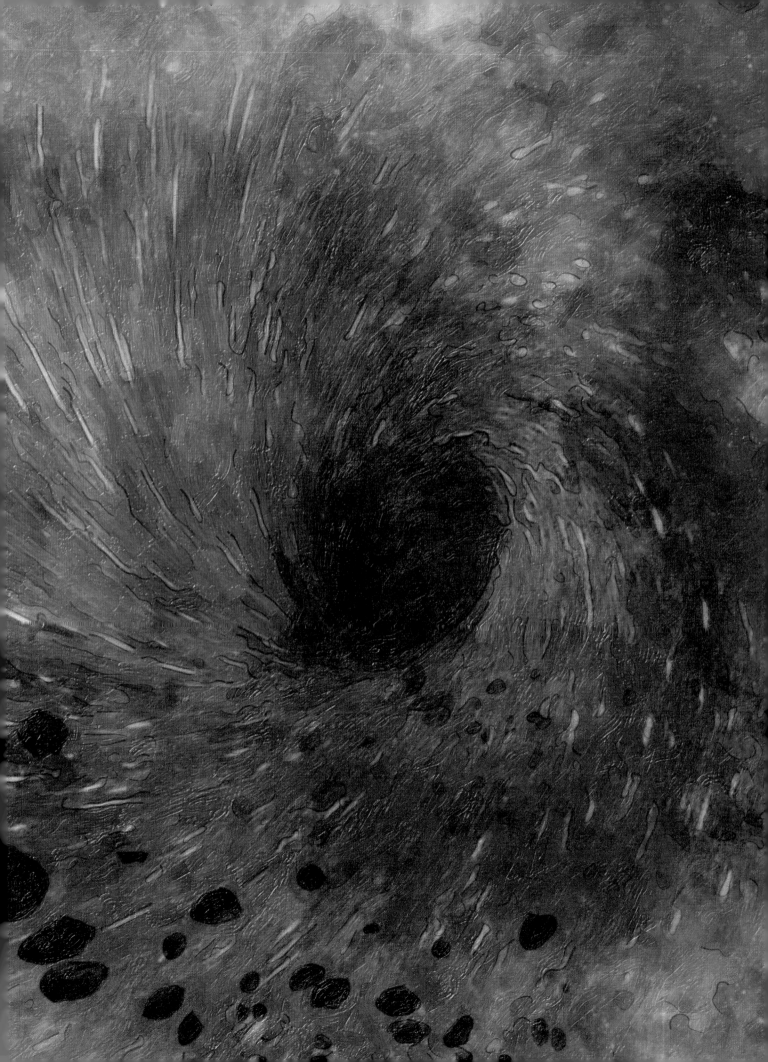

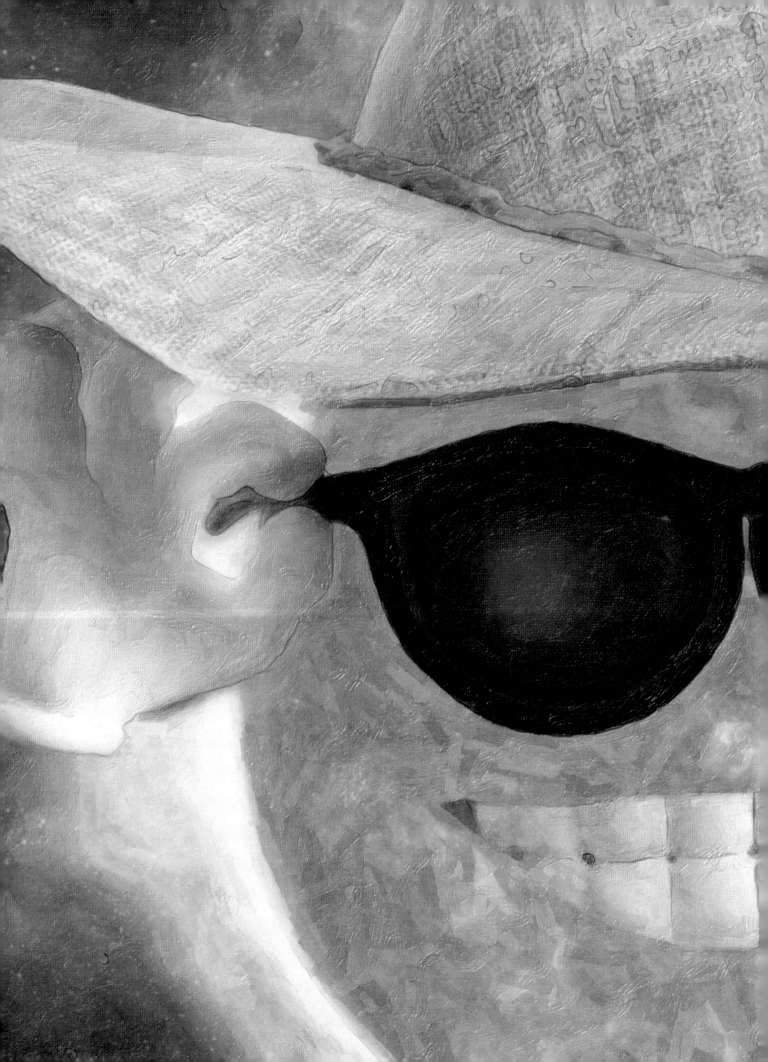

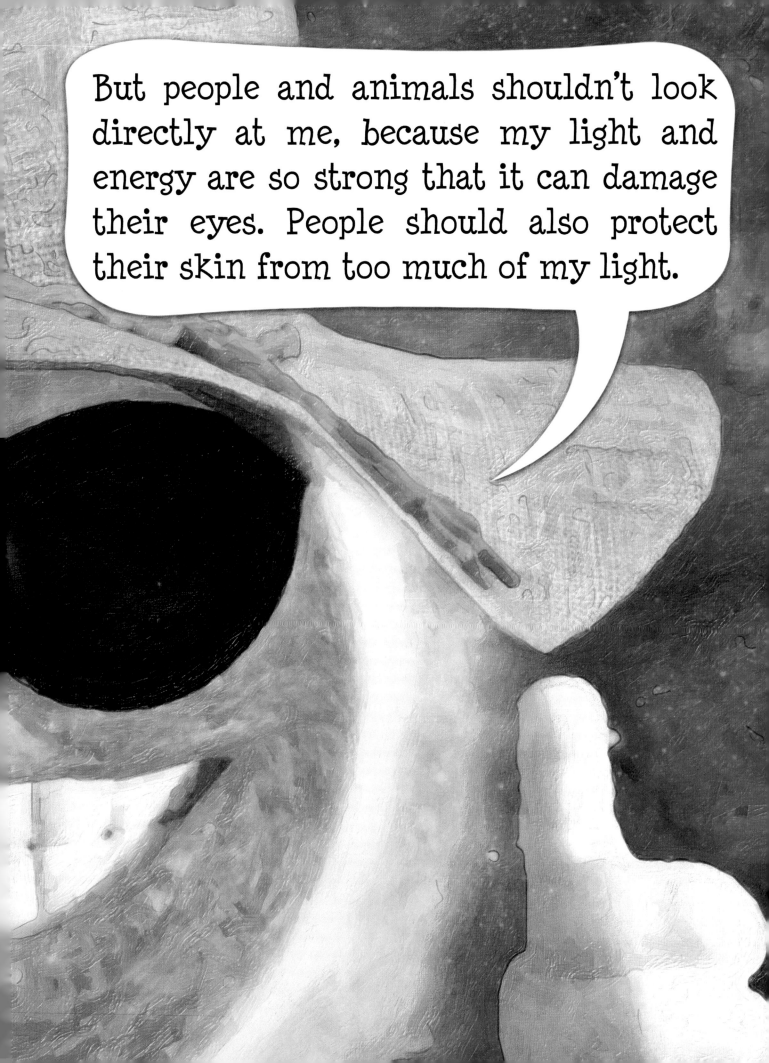

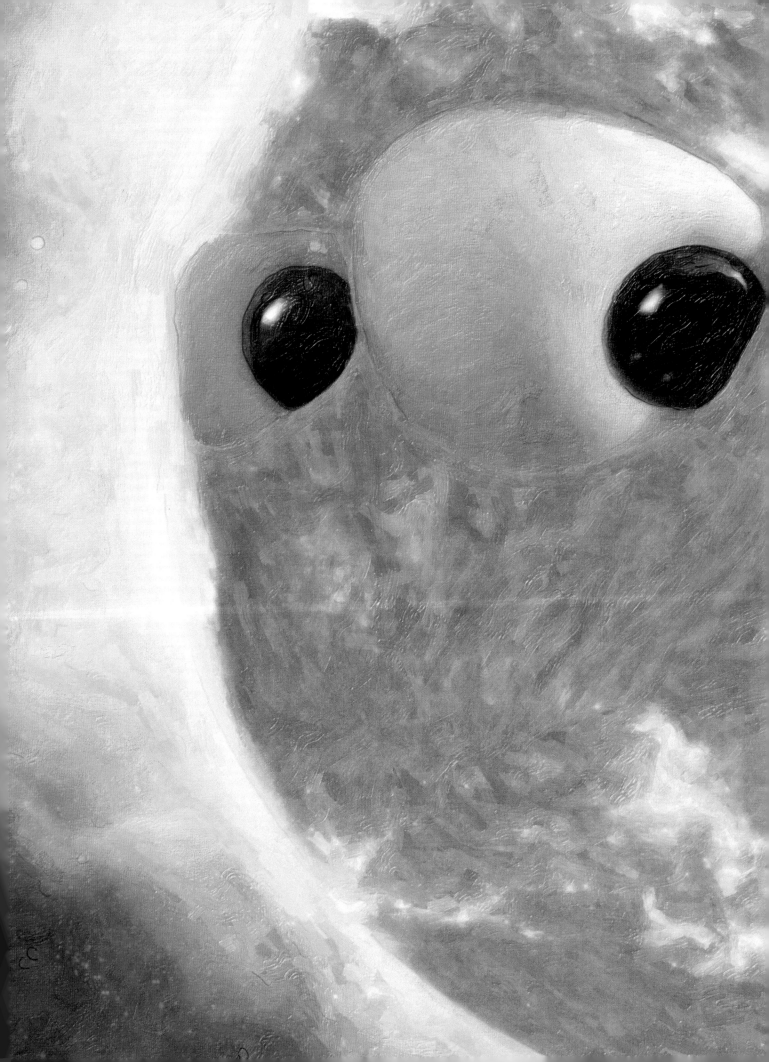

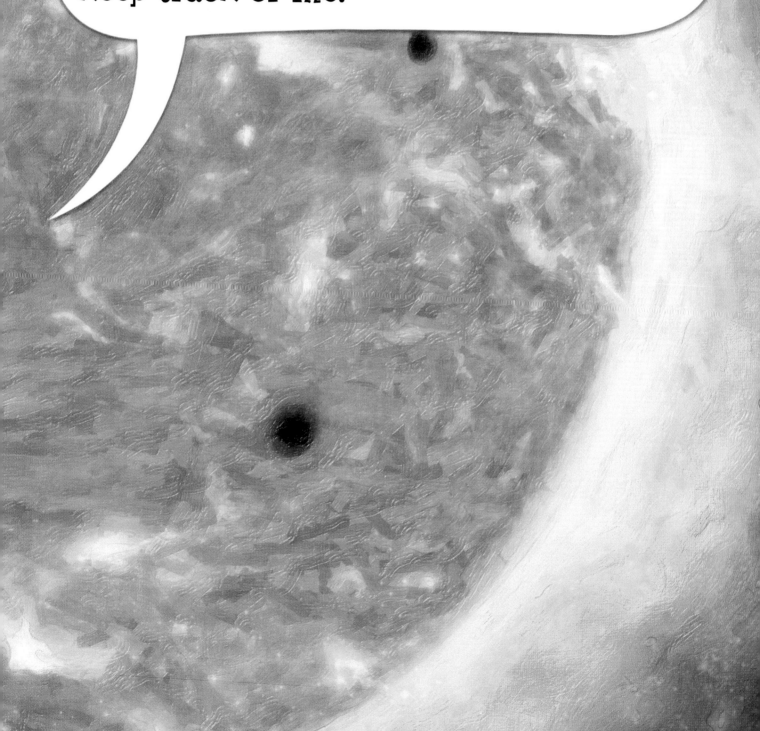

I'm so big that even small sunspots on my surface can cause big bursts of energy. Sunspots are darker, cooler spots that move around or even disappear and then come back. Scientists use them to keep track of me.

Sometimes my sunspots explode with energy that can shoot way out into space. If it's a big enough explosion, people on Earth see it as colorful lights in the night sky called an aurora.

Just remember, even on the cloudiest of days, I'm still shining bright way up high. You can count on me to fill your days with warmth and light!

Why is it so important to protect your eyes and skin from the Sun?

Why isn't there life on the planets closest to the Sun?

Why can't scientists land spaceships or rovers on the Sun?

Why do scientists like to watch and keep track of what's happening on the Sun's surface?

ISBN: 978-1-950553-02-0

First House of Lore paperback edition, 2019

Visit us at www.HouseOfLore.net

I Am Earth
Rebecca and James McDonald

I Am the Moon
REBECCA AND JAMES MCDONALD

I Am the Solar System
REBECCA AND JAMES MCDONALD

I Am Mars
REBECCA AND JAMES MCDONALD

I Am Spring
REBECCA AND JAMES MCDONALD

I Am A Bee
REBECCA

I Am A Dinosaur

I Am Tyrannosaurus Rex

I Am Triceratops

I Am A Frog

Bo the Bear BUILDS a Monster Truck
REBECCA AND JAMES MCDONALD

Bo the Bear BUILDS a Race Car
REBECCA AND JAMES MCDONALD

Why Mama Why

Rainy Day Poems

The Little Unicorn That Had No Horn

The Scribbles
REBECCA AND JAMES MCDONALD

Through The Milky Way On A PB&J
James McDonald

Tra...

A...

WILFORD AND BLUE
THE Kite Calamity
REBECCA AND JAMES MCDONALD

Petey And The Bee
A Dog's Tale
Rebecca and James McDonald

Do I Look Odd To You
Rebecca and James McDonald

A...
Rebecca and James McDonald

James McDonald

Rebecca and James McD

Made in the USA
Las Vegas, NV
05 June 2021